clap your hands!

stomp your feet!

If you're happy
and you know it

HOo

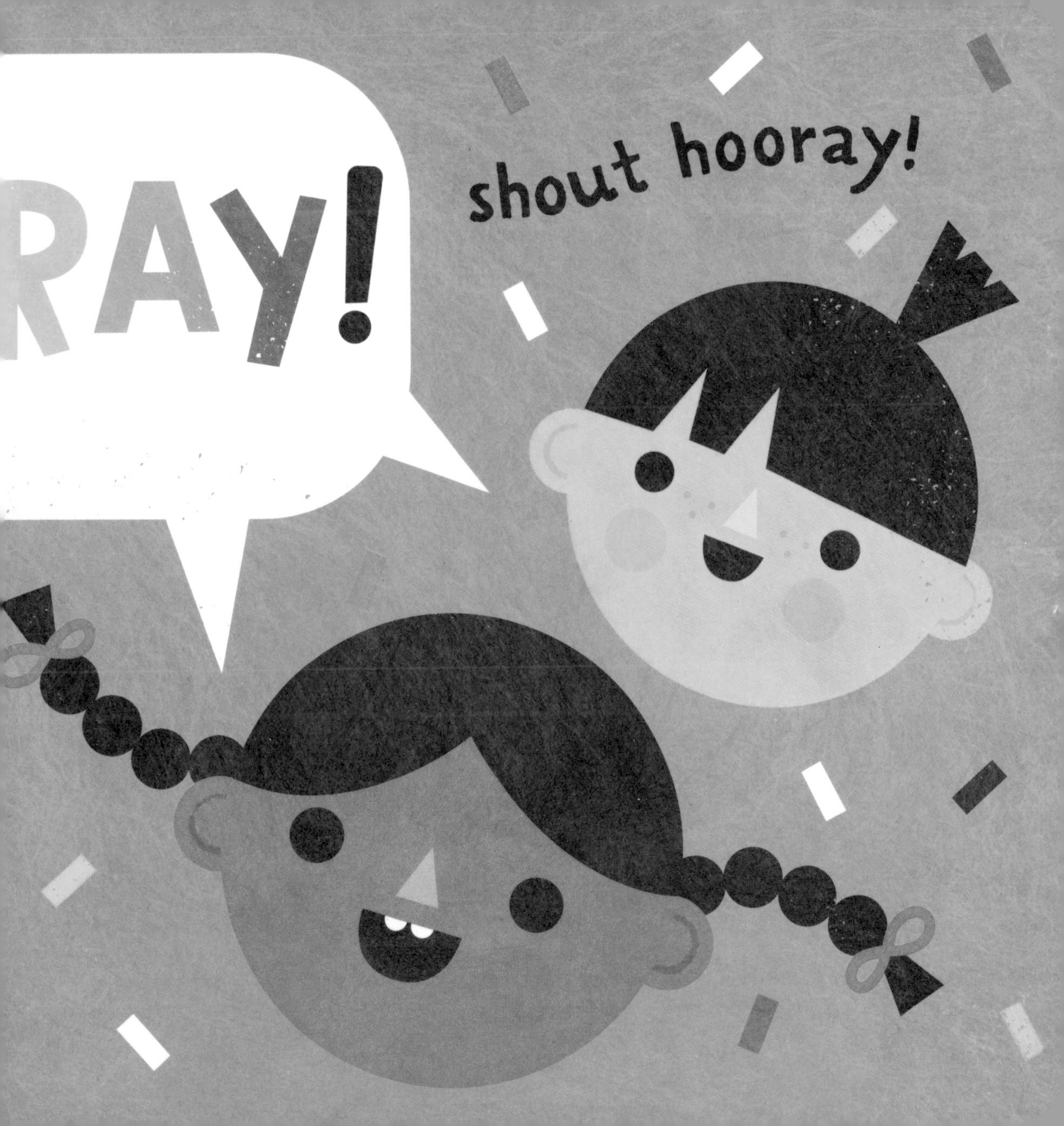
RAY!
shout hooray!

If you're happy
and you know it

then your face
will really show it!

For ages 0 and up

BOOKS BABIES CAN REALLY SINK THEIR GUMS INTO!

If you're happy and you know it, clap your hands! *Clap, clap!*
If you're happy and you know it, stomp your feet! *Stomp, stomp!*
If you're happy and you know it, shout hooray! *HOORAY!*

Teach baby the beloved song in a book that's INDESTRUCTIBLE.

Dear Parents: INDESTRUCTIBLES are built for the way babies "read": with their hands and mouths. INDESTRUCTIBLES won't rip or tear and are 100% washable. They're made for baby to hold, grab, chew, pull, and bend.

← CHEW ALL THESE AND MORE!

$5.95 US   ISBN 978-1-5235-1415-1

Library of Congress Cataloging-in-Publication Data is available.
WORKMAN is a registered trademark of Workman Publishing Co., Inc.
First printing July 2021 | 10 9 8 7 6 5 4 3 2 1

All INDESTRUCTIBLES books have been safety-tested and meet or exceed ASTM-F963 and CPSIA guidelines. INDESTRUCTIBLES is a registered trademark of Indestructibles, LLC. Contact specialmarkets@workman.com regarding special discounts for bulk purchases.
Printed in China

WORKMAN PUBLISHING CO., INC. 225 Varick Street, New York, NY 10014 • indestructiblesinc.com